THE MOUNT EVEREST DISASTER OF 1996

by Cindy L. Rodriguez • illustrated by Paul McCaffrey

CAPSTONE PRESS
a capstone imprint

Published by Capstone Press, an imprint of Capstone
1710 Roe Crest Drive, North Mankato, Minnesota 56003
capstonepub.com

Library of Congress Cataloging-in-Publication Data is available on the Library of
Congress website.

ISBN: 9781666390469 (hardcover)
ISBN: 9781666390414 (paperback)
ISBN: 9781666390421 (ebook PDF)

Summary: On May 6, 1996, dozens of excited people set off to climb Mount Everest.
On the morning of May 10, the skies were clear. The summit was in sight. But hours
later, a terrible storm hit. Eight climbers died when they became trapped near the
peak. What went wrong, and how did the survivors make it back alive?

Editorial Credits
Editor: Abby Huff; Designer: Dina Her; Production Specialist: Tori Abraham

All internet sites appearing in back matter were available and accurate when this
book was sent to press.

Direct quotations appear in bold italicized text on the following pages:
Pages 7, 8, 9, 10, 23: from *Into Thin Air: A Personal Account of the Mount Everest
Disaster* by Jon Krakauer. New York: Villard, 1997.
Pages 12, 13: from *Left for Dead: My Journey Home from Everest* by Beck Weathers
with Stephen G. Michaud. New York: Villard, 2000.

TABLE OF CONTENTS

Reaching the top of Mount Everest puts you at the highest point on Earth—if you survive the climb.

Everest sits on the border of China and Nepal. Its peak is 29,032 feet above sea level. Breathing at such extreme heights is difficult. The air is thin. At about 26,000 feet, the human body begins to shut down from lack of oxygen. This altitude and above is called the Death Zone.

Despite the dangers, more than 500 people try to climb Everest each year.

On May 6, 1996, dozens of excited climbers started their journey. They set off from Base Camp at the bottom of the mountain.

Here we go!

On the morning of May 10, the summit was in sight. The day was cold and windy. But the skies were clear.

It's more beautiful than I imagined!

We're almost there!

Hours later, a terrible storm hit. Eight climbers died. At the time, it was the worst loss of life on Everest in a single event. What went wrong?

April 12, 1996

Rob Hall was an expert climber. His company, Adventure Consultants, led people up Everest for up to $65,000 each.

Welcome to Base Camp! Come on in and rest.

That year, Rob had eight paying clients. Among them were:

Jon Krakauer, an American journalist for *Outside* magazine and experienced climber.

Doug Hansen, a U.S. postal worker who had almost made it to the top of Everest the previous year.

Yasuko Namba, a Japanese business person who had climbed the highest mountain on six other continents.

Beck Weathers, a doctor from Texas.

I'm back!

Hey, Rob! Happy to be here!

Say hello to guides Mike Groom and Andy Harris. And that's Ang Dorje, my head Sherpa.

Sherpas are important to Everest climbing teams. These local experts carry gear, set up ropes, and place extra oxygen bottles along the route.

Another climbing company called Mountain Madness was run by Scott Fischer. He also had eight clients that year.

Rob and Scott were competitors, but they would try for the summit together. Each man had a journalist in their group. Stories of a successful climb would be good for business.

Many other groups were also at Base Camp. They all hoped to go up Everest. "Summit Fever," as it was called, brought in climbers of all kinds. Some had little experience.

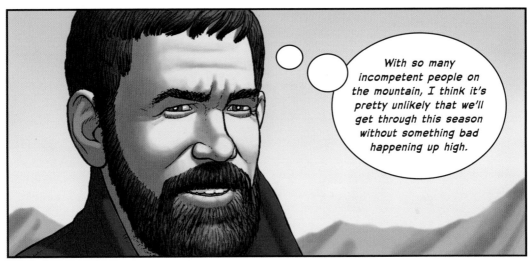

With so many incompetent people on the mountain, I think it's pretty unlikely that we'll get through this season without something bad happening up high.

For weeks, Rob's and Scott's teams trained. They climbed to resting points on the mountain called Camps 1, 2, and 3. Then they returned to Base Camp. These trips helped their bodies get used to the thin air.

Easy, Beck. When we get through the Khumbu Icefall, we'll reach Camp 1.

What is that?

I think it was a Sherpa who died three years ago.

On the climb to Camp 2, the group came across a reminder of how dangerous Everest could be. The bodies of those who die climbing are often left there. It can be risky to remove them.

After returning from Camp 2, clients were feeling the effects of the thin air. Some had lost weight. Others had headaches and nasty coughs.

It feels like somebody's driven a nail between my eyes.

Before the big climb, Rob reminded his clients of the turnaround time. When they went for the summit, they needed to turn back by 2 p.m. After that, they'd risk losing oxygen in the Death Zone.

Any idiot can get up this hill. The trick is to get back down alive.

We're ready, boss!

At 4:30 a.m. on May 6, 1996, Rob's and Scott's teams left Base Camp. It was the start of a five-day climb to the top of Mount Everest.

Everest is calling!

Let's do this!

To the Summit

It feels good to be on our way to the summit, yeah?

Yeah!

The teams reached Camp 2. They were now at 21,600 feet. They had a rest day on May 7.

How are you feeling, Doug?

My throat still hurts, but *I've put too much of myself into this mountain to quit now, without giving it everything I've got.*

On the morning of May 8, a windstorm ripped through camp. Rob and Scott agreed to wait before heading out.

AGH!

The winds settled, and the teams continued on. Not far from Camp 3, a rock fell from the cliffs.

Andy! Are you all right?

I might be a bit stiff, but that's it.

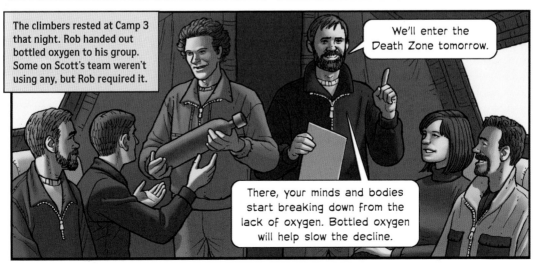

The climbers rested at Camp 3 that night. Rob handed out bottled oxygen to his group. Some on Scott's team weren't using any, but Rob required it.

We'll enter the Death Zone tomorrow.

There, your minds and bodies start breaking down from the lack of oxygen. Bottled oxygen will help slow the decline.

On May 9, the teams made it to Camp 4. Another powerful windstorm hit. If it continued, the teams wouldn't be able to climb farther up.

This is déjà vu, man.

You're right, Scott! Let's see if Mother Nature calms down.

The winds did calm. Around 11:30 p.m., Rob's team set off for the final push to the summit. Scott's team followed half an hour later. Groups from Taiwan and South Africa would go next.

Saddle up! We're going for it!

Three hours later, one of Rob's clients stepped out of line.

Hey, Frank, are you okay?

Something just doesn't feel right. I'm going back.

Soon after, Doug Hansen stepped out of line too.

Doug, are you okay?

I'm cold and don't feel good. I'm heading down.

When Rob reached his client, the two talked briefly. Nobody knows what was said. But afterward, Doug started back toward the summit.

By 7:30 a.m. on May 10, the groups were near the Balcony. This area is about 1,500 feet below the summit. But Beck Weathers could no longer see. The thin air was affecting his vision.

Rob, cross my heart, hope to die, I'm sticking.

...promise me that you're going to stay here until I come back.

The others went on. But they soon had to stop when they saw ropes had not been fixed. Fixed ropes are anchored along the route. They help people climb safely.

Why aren't the ropes fixed?

I don't know, Neal.

The teams had planned for Sherpas to leave early to fix the ropes. It's not clear why they didn't. Some said Ang didn't get along with Scott's head Sherpa. He was tired of doing most of the work.

Ang, are you going to fix the ropes?

No.

The guides set the ropes themselves. As they did, a crowd of climbers grew. Members of the Taiwanese and South African teams caught up to Rob's and Scott's. Everyone had to wait.

This isn't good. Now there's going to be a bottleneck!

Climbers started up again once the ropes were ready. But some from Rob's team decided continuing was too risky.

There are so many people.

It's already midday.

We won't be able to reach the summit before the 2 p.m. turnaround time. Let's go back.

Around 1:30 p.m., the first climbers from Rob's and Scott's teams reached the summit of Mount Everest.

We did it!

One by one, more team members reached the summit. After celebrating, they climbed down. People from the Taiwanese and South African groups came up too. With the "traffic jam" of climbers, it was slow going up and down.

The 2 p.m. turnaround time arrived. But climbers didn't turn back. Some were still pushing forward. Others waited on the summit for them.

Base Camp, this is Rob. Doug is just coming up.

I'll head down right after.

By 3:10 p.m., Mountain Madness guide Neal Beidleman started down with four clients. They passed Scott struggling upward.

Scott's a pro. He'll probably tag the summit and catch up.

Scott reached the summit around 3:30 p.m. About the same time, the clear skies started becoming cloudy.

Scott, please, let's go down fast.

Base Camp, we all made it! Ugh, I'm tired.

Others left, but Rob stayed to wait for Doug. When he saw Doug coming up, Rob helped his client to the top. They reached it at about 4 p.m. It was two hours past the turnaround time.

The two started down. At this point, anyone on the mountain was at great risk. The climb had left them exhausted. Their oxygen was low from being in the Death Zone so long. Now, the weather was turning.

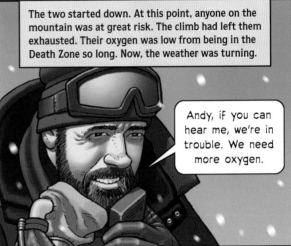

Andy, if you can hear me, we're in trouble. We need more oxygen.

Andy went back. But the guide was likely low on oxygen too. He was also going into an unexpected storm. There's evidence Andy made it to Rob, but it's not clear what happened after that. Andy was never seen again. He was presumed dead.

Others would also not survive the next hours.

Other members from Rob's and Scott's teams made their way down to Camp 4. As they did, a fast-moving storm hit the mountain. They headed right into hurricane-strength winds.

Many people were low on oxygen because of the earlier delays. They were weak and tired. Now the incoming storm created an even more dangerous situation.

In Neal's group, client Sandy Hill Pittman collapsed.

Sandy!

Another client gave Sandy a steroid shot. It helped fight the effects of the thin air. But it was a short-term fix.

We have to keep moving!

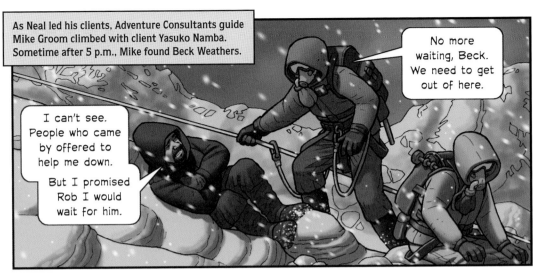

As Neal led his clients, Adventure Consultants guide Mike Groom climbed with client Yasuko Namba. Sometime after 5 p.m., Mike found Beck Weathers.

No more waiting, Beck. We need to get out of here.

I can't see. People who came by offered to help me down.

But I promised Rob I would wait for him.

Meanwhile, Rob and Doug were stuck near the summit. Around 5:15 p.m., Rob radioed his Base Camp team.

Doug is out of oxygen. He can't move.

Go alone to Camp 4, Rob. You can help rescue Doug tomorrow.

I'm not leaving him.

Scott and Sherpa Lopsang were also near the mountaintop. Scott was exhausted and unable to move. The leader of the Taiwanese group, Makalu Gau, soon stumbled into the area.

I'm sick. I'm sick . . .

I can't go any farther.

Oh, Scott! Rest here and I'll go for help.

Neal's and Mike's groups met up. The storm worsened. After 6 p.m., they couldn't see through the blowing snow. The windchill had plunged to minus 140 degrees Fahrenheit. Around 10 p.m., they decided to stop wandering blindly.

Huddle up! We're going to wait for a break in the storm!

Keep moving your arms and legs!

Mike was able to use his radio. He spoke with clients who were already at Camp 4.

I think we're close to camp, but I need help with directions.

We're banging pots and flashing lights for you, Mike!

People at Camp 4 tried to help. But the lost climbers couldn't see or hear anything.

Later, the sky cleared just enough. The lost climbers got a sense for where they were. Those who had the strength decided to keep going.

We have to make a run for Camp 4.

I agree. If we don't get help, we'll all die.

Around 12:45 a.m. on May 11, Neal, Mike, and two clients stumbled into the camp.

The others... need help!

I got back long ago. I'm rested. I can go.

Mountain Madness guide Anatoli Boukreev managed to find the lost clients. He carried one person to camp. Then he came back for two more people. He left Beck and Yasuko.

With the storm still raging, Anatoli had to focus on those he thought could be saved.

What about Beck and Yasuko?

They are dead or close to it. We will send people later to check.

On the morning of May 11, the worst of the storm was over. Rob radioed around 4:45 a.m. He was near the South Summit. He couldn't move from lack of oxygen and frostbite. He reported that Doug was gone.

By midmorning, Neal started leading clients down the mountain. Rescuers set out to search for survivors. Sherpas got about 328 feet away from Rob. But high winds were still a problem.

We must turn back!

Sherpas found Scott and Makalu. Both were near dead. The Sherpas focused on saving Makalu, who was awake. They left Scott with a tank of oxygen in case he woke. He never did.

Rescuers checked Beck and Yasuko. It seemed both had died. They were left in the snow.

But around 4 p.m., Beck did wake. His teammates were stunned when he staggered into Camp 4. His hands and nose were black with frostbite.

At 6:20 p.m. on May 11, Base Camp radioed Rob. They connected him to his pregnant wife, Jan, in New Zealand.

I'm sending all my positive energy your way!

I love you. Sleep well, my sweetheart.

Please don't worry too much.

Those were Rob Hall's last words. His body remains on Mount Everest.

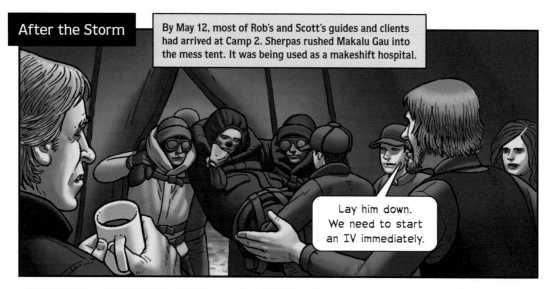

After the Storm

By May 12, most of Rob's and Scott's guides and clients had arrived at Camp 2. Sherpas rushed Makalu Gau into the mess tent. It was being used as a makeshift hospital.

Lay him down. We need to start an IV immediately.

This is the worst frostbite I've ever seen.

Later that day, Beck was also brought to Camp 2.

Your frostbite is even worse than Makalu's!

On May 13, the Nepalese Army sent a rescue helicopter for Makalu. It landed at nearly 20,000 feet. A helicopter had never landed that high on Everest before. A half hour later, it returned for Beck. Both men were rushed to the hospital.

The same day, the surviving Adventure Consultants and Mountain Madness climbers returned to Base Camp.

Welcome back.

May you all rest in peace. We'll miss you.

The survivors held a memorial service in honor of their friends. Afterward, it was time to return home and heal. Guide Mike and client Charlotte Fox were taken by helicopter to be treated for frostbite. Others needed basic medical attention. But they would all face reporters, grieving families of those who had died, and traumatic memories for years to come.

At the time, May 10–11, 1996, was the deadliest event on Mount Everest. A total of eight people lost their lives.

Rob Hall, owner of Adventure Consultants. He was an expert climber from New Zealand. He reached the Everest summit five times. Rob's wife, Jan, gave birth to their daughter two months after Rob died.

Scott Fischer, owner of Mountain Madness. He was a skilled American climber. He first reached the top of Everest in 1994 without using extra oxygen.

Doug Hansen, Adventure Consultants client. He was a U.S. postal worker. He had been climbing for 12 years.

Yasuko Namba, Adventure Consultants client. She was a business person from Japan. When she got to the top of Everest, she became the second Japanese woman to climb the highest peak on each continent.

Andy Harris, Adventure Consultants guide. He was born in England but lived in New Zealand. His climb up Everest was his first summit attempt.

Rob's and Scott's teams climbed the South Summit. At the same time, a group called the Indo-Tibetan Border Police was climbing the north side of Everest.

When the storm started, some of the men turned back. But Tsewang Smanla, Dorje Morup, and Tsewang Paljor kept going. They did not survive.

MAP OF THE EXPEDITION

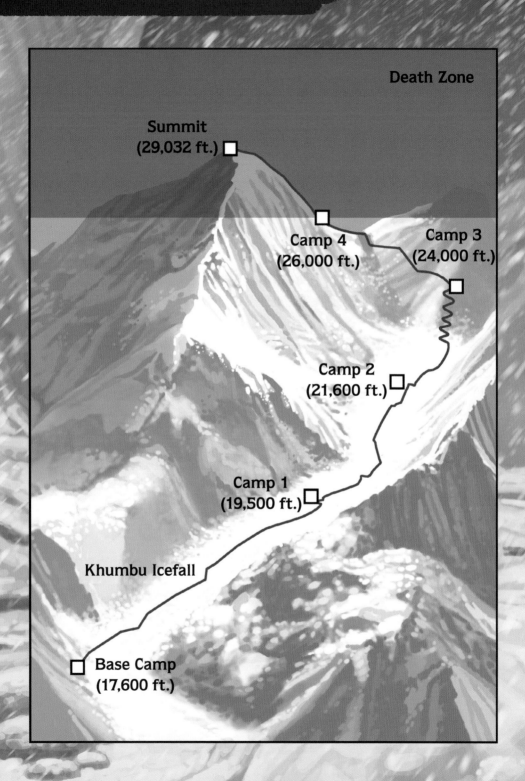

Death Zone

Summit
(29,032 ft.)

Camp 4
(26,000 ft.)

Camp 3
(24,000 ft.)

Camp 2
(21,600 ft.)

Camp 1
(19,500 ft.)

Khumbu Icefall

Base Camp
(17,600 ft.)

MORE ABOUT THE EXPEDITION

Two tragic events happened even before the fierce storm hit Mount Everest. In April 1996, a Sherpa who worked for Scott Fischer was helping to prepare the camps along the mountain. His name was Ngawang Topche. He was carrying up supplies. One day, he was found sitting on the ice 21,000 feet above sea level. He had been feeling weak and short of breath. When the Sherpa came back down to Base Camp, he was stumbling and coughing up blood. He had developed a life-threatening illness caused by the high altitude. A helicopter rescue took him off the mountain so he could be treated. But the Sherpa died from the illness on June 9.

The second tragedy happened on the morning of May 9. The Taiwanese team was preparing to climb to Camp 4. Member Chen Yu-Nan crawled out of his tent. But he hadn't put crampons on his boots. These metal spikes help climbers not to slip on ice and snow. Chen slid headfirst into a crevasse. Others pulled him out, but he died from injuries later that day.

Climbers Beck Weathers and Makalu Gau both survived the 1996 disaster. But they faced long roads to recovery. Each had extreme cases of frostbite. Makalu lost all his fingers and toes. Beck's right arm was removed halfway between the elbow and wrist. He lost the fingers on his left hand. Through many surgeries, doctors rebuilt his nose.

GLOSSARY

altitude (AL-tih-tood)—the height of something above sea level or above Earth's surface

client (KLAHY-uhnt)—someone who uses the services of a company or a professional person

collapse (kuh-LAPS)—to fall suddenly from being ill or weak

decline (dih-KLAHYN)—the process of becoming weaker or worse off

delay (dih-LEY)—the act of making something happen more slowly than normal

exhausted (eg-ZAWS-ted)—very tired and completely out of mental and/or physical energy

fixed rope (FIKSD ROHP)—a rope that is firmly bolted into rock or ice in order to help climbers safely move through an area

frostbite (FRAWST-bahyt)—the freezing of skin on some part of the body due to cold temperatures

Sherpa (SHER-puh)—a person native to the Himalayas; Sherpas are known for helping people climb the mountains

steroid (STER-oid)—a chemical that is made by the body or created as a drug; climbers sometimes take steroids to treat the effects of being in high altitudes

summit (SUHM-it)—the highest point of a mountain

traumatic (truh-MAT-ik)—upsetting and causing a lot of stress

READ MORE

Mavrikis, Peter. *Explorers of the Highest Places on Earth.* North Mankato, MN: Capstone, 2021.

Purja, Nimsdai. *Beyond Possible: Young Readers' Edition.* Washington, D.C.: National Geographic Kids, 2022.

Stewart, Alexandra. *Everest: The Remarkable Story of Edmund Hillary and Tenzing Norgay.* New York: Bloomsbury, 2020.

INTERNET SITES

Easy Science for Kids: Mount Everest
easyscienceforkids.com/all-about-mount-everest/

Frontline: Storm Over Everest
pbs.org/wgbh/pages/frontline/everest/

National Geographic: Expedition Everest
nationalgeographic.org/interactive/expedition-everest/

AUTHOR BIO

Cindy L. Rodriguez is the author of the YA novel *When Reason Breaks* and has contributed to the anthology *Life Inside My Mind: 31 Authors Share Their Personal Struggles*. She has also written the text for *Volleyball Ace*, *Drill Team Determination*, and *Gymnastics Payback*, all part of the Jake Maddox series. Before becoming a teacher, she was an award-winning reporter for *The Hartford Courant* and researcher for *The Boston Globe's* Spotlight Team. She is a founder of Latinxs in Kid Lit, a blog that celebrates children's literature by/for/about Latinxs. Cindy is a big fan of the three Cs: coffee, chocolate, and coconut. She is currently a middle school reading specialist in Connecticut, where she lives with her family.

ILLUSTRATOR BIO

Paul McCaffrey is a freelance illustrator, mainly in the area of children's education. His clients have included NME, Vox, Punch, Deadline, Empire, CUP, OUP, Attack! Books, Macmillan, Harcourt, and Heinemann, amongst others. More recently, he has drawn comics for Marvel, DC, IDW, Thinkable, and Network Distribution. For Titan Comics, he has produced a number of covers as well as drawing *Anno Dracula 1895: Seven Days in Mayhem* and co-creating *Adler* with Lavie Tidhar. He lives in the UK with his wife and cat and far too many books than is good for him.